Economic Crisis, Quality of Work, an

Economic Crisis, Quality of Work, and Social Integration

The European Experience

Edited by
Duncan Gallie

OXFORD
UNIVERSITY PRESS

OXFORD
UNIVERSITY PRESS

Great Clarendon Street, Oxford, OX2 6DP,
United Kingdom

Oxford University Press is a department of the University of Oxford.
It furthers the University's objective of excellence in research, scholarship,
and education by publishing worldwide. Oxford is a registered trade mark of
Oxford University Press in the UK and in certain other countries

Published in the United States of America by Oxford University Press
198 Madison Avenue, New York, NY 10016, United States of America

British Library Cataloguing in Publication Data
Data available

Library of Congress Control Number: 2013938044

ISBN 978–0–19–966471–9 (Hbk.)
ISBN 978–0–19–966472–6 (Pbk.)

Printed and bound in Great Britain by
CPI Group (UK) Ltd, Croydon, CR0 4YY

To the late Roger Jowell
whose vision, enthusiasm and energy ensured
the success of the European Social Survey

Acknowledgements

This book emerges from an initiative originally taken by a research group within the Economic Life, Quality of Work and Social Cohesion (EQUALSOC) Network of Excellence, funded between 2005 and 2010 as part of the EU's Sixth Framework Programme. Several of the group's members were involved in the construction of the 2004 module of the European Social Survey (ESS), which focused on the Family, Work, and Well-Being. With the onset of economic crisis, we felt that there was a powerful case to replicate the key elements of that survey and this resulted in 2010 in the first 'repeat' module in the life of the ESS. We worked very closely throughout with the ESS's Central Coordination Team at City University and are particularly grateful to Roger Jowell, Rory Fitzgerald, and Eric Harrison for their support and input into the project. We are also very grateful to the British Academy for making it possible to continue meeting as a research team to analyse and discuss the results of the survey, as a result of an award from its Small Grants Scheme.

Although the core evidence on which the analyses are based are the 2004 and 2010 waves of the European Social Survey, we also have made extensive use of data from the yearly European Union Labour Force Surveys (EULFS) from 2004 to 2010, to which, as members of the EQUALSOC network, we had access at a relatively early point in time. We are particularly grateful to Roxane Silberman for her work in negotiating that access on behalf of the members of the Network and to Eurostat for agreeing to grant it. Eurostat, however, has no responsibility for the results and conclusions, which are purely the responsibility of the research team.

A number of people have played an invaluable role in helping to prepare the data. Hande Inanc carried out the work of linking the 2004 and 2010 data, as well as assisting other team members with runs from the EULFS. We owe a considerable debt to Dorothy Watson for her work in reweighting both of the ESS surveys in the light of data from the EULFS. Jane Roberts, the data officer at Nuffield College, was a great help in the acquisition of the EULFS data and the management of its contracts. I am also very grateful to Yanislava Moyse for her wonderfully efficient assistance in the management of both the EQUALSOC and the British Academy grants and to Sarah Wilkins-Laflamme for her willingness to spend a significant part of her Christmas

putting together the references of the book and for her work in compiling the index. Finally, my thanks to the staff at Oxford University Press for their support of the project and their work in preparing the publication of the book.

Duncan Gallie
Nuffield College, Oxford

Contents

List of Figures   xi
List of Tables   xvii
List of Abbreviations   xxi
List of Contributors   xxiii

1. Economic Crisis, the Quality of Work, and Social Integration:
   Issues and Context   1
   Duncan Gallie

2. Economic Crisis and Employment Change: The Great Regression   30
   Michael Tåhlin

3. Distribution in the Downturn   58
   Michael Tåhlin

4. Continuing Training in Times of Economic Crisis   88
   Martina Dieckhoff

5. Job Control, Work Intensity, and Work Stress   115
   Duncan Gallie and Ying Zhou

6. Insecurity and the Peripheral Workforce   142
   Vanessa Gash and Hande Inanc

7. Work–Family Conflict and Economic Change   169
   Frances McGinnity and Helen Russell

8. Economic Downturn and Work Motivation   195
   Nadia Steiber

9. Unemployment and Subjective Well-Being   229
   Helen Russell, Dorothy Watson, and Frances McGinnity

10. Economic Crisis, Political Legitimacy, and Social Cohesion   256
    Javier Polavieja

11. Economic Crisis, Country Variations, and Institutional Structure   279
    Duncan Gallie

Contents

List of Figures

1.1 Percentage decline of GDP per capita from 2008 to (a) year of recession trough and (b) 2010   4

1.2 Unemployment rates 2007–2010   5

1.3 Changes in unemployment rates 2004–2010   6

1.4 Net reductions in workforce reported by employees   7

1.5 Bargaining coordination 2000–2009   20

1.6 Bargaining coverage and union density   22

2.1 Employment fall 2007/8–2010 in 18 European countries. Percentage points, summary indicator of employment and unemployment   37

2.2 Comparative economic growth 1990–2010. GDP/capita in constant prices, 1990 = 100   38

2.3 Comparative growth of construction industry employment, 2000–2010, 2000 = 100   40

2.4 Predicted (from Table 2.1) and actual employment change 2007/8–2010   41

2.5 Equality-promoting institutions and economic wealth   44

2.6 Equality-promoting institutional structure net of economic wealth   46

2.7 Employment fall 2007/8–2010 by equality-promoting institutions   47

2.8 Volatility-predicted employment fall 2007/8–2010 by equality-promoting institutions   48

2.9 Excess (given volatility) employment fall 2007/8–2010 by equality-promoting institutions   49

2.10 Rates of job separation and job finding one year prior to the start of recession   51

2.11 Rates of job separation and job finding between 2008 and 2009   52

2.12 Changes in job finding and job separation rates from 2006–7 / 2007–8 to 2008–9   53

2.13 Two dimensions of labour market institutions: equality and flexibility   54

2.14   Excess (given volatility) employment fall in recession
        by labour market flexibility   56

3.1   Employment (age 20–64) and unemployment
        (harmonized) rates, averages 2000–2007   60

3.2   Employment index (employment rate minus
        unemployment rate) by country, average 2000–2007   61

3.3   Employment rates by gender, averages 2000–2007   62

3.4   Male unemployment rates by age, averages 2000–2007   63

3.5   Male employment rates by age, averages 2000–2007   64

3.6   Employment rates by education, averages 2000–2007   64

3.7   Employment fall 2007/8–2010 by gender, age, and education
        (percentage point differences between time-points);
        18 countries, unweighted averages   66

3.8   Employment fall 2007/8–2010 by gender and regime
        (percentage point differences between time-points)   67

3.9   Employment fall 2007/8–2010 by age and regime
        (percentage point differences between time-points)   68

3.10   Employment fall 2007/8–2010 by education and
        regime (percentage point differences between time-points)   69

3.11   Fall in gender employment gap 2007/8–2010 by
        total employment decline   70

3.12   Residual employment loss 2007/8–2010 by institutional
        structure. Correlations between five employment gaps
        (by gender, age and education) and two dimensions of
        labour market institutions (equality and flexibility)   72

3.13   Levels of occupational skill and population
        education, averages 2000–2007 (scale 0–100)   75

3.14   Occupational skill level (scale 0–100) and economic
        wealth (GDP/capita), averages 2000–2007   76

3.15   Rise in average education (scale 0–100) among employed
        population (age 25–64) from 2007/8 to 2010 by size of total
        employment decline   77

3.16   Rise in average occupational skill level (scale 0–100) from
        2007/8 to 2010 by size of total employment decline   78

3.17   Change in occupational skill upgrading from 2004–2007
        to 2007–2010 by total employment decline   79

3.18   Changes in employment size by occupation (per cent)
        and correlations with total employment change 2007/8–2010   81

3.19   Change in occupational polarization (scale 0–100)
        2007/8–2010 by total employment decline   82

3.20 Changes in occupational structure (skill rise, polarization, and occupational category size) 2007/8–2010 by labour market institutions (equality and flexibility) 83

4.1 Time trends 2004–2010: continuing training amongst the dependently employed by country 99

4.2 Temporal change in continuing training and change in GDP growth 102

5.1 Employees' job control 2004–2010 117

5.2 Job control by occupational class 2004–2010 119

5.3 Ratios of job control scores of higher managers and professionals compared to routine employees by country group 120

5.4 Influence of employee representatives by country (employee reports) 128

5.5 Influence of representatives in the workplace and individual job control 129

5.6 Bargaining coordination and influence of workplace representation 131

5.7 Trade union density and influence of workplace representatives 131

5.8 Work intensity and occupational class 2004–2010 134

5.9 Work intensity, firm vulnerability, and individual change in job security 135

5.10 Job strain types and life satisfaction 136

5.11 Job strain types by country group, 2004 137

5.12 Change in proportion of high strain jobs 2004–2010 138

6.1 Growth of atypical work in Europe 1990–2007 144

6.2 Temporary and involuntary temporary work among employees 2004–2010 146

6.3 Part-time and involuntary part-time work among employees 2004–2010 146

6.4 Level of employment protection in OECD and selected non-OECD countries 2008 149

6.5 Change in the proportion of temporary employees 2008–2010 150

6.6 Change in the proportion of part-time employees 2008–2010 151

6.7 Share of temporary employees among occupational classes 2008–2010 153

6.8 Share of part-time employees among occupational classes 2008–2010 154

6.9 Change in unemployment and temporary employment 2008–2010 157

6.10	Decomposition employment change by contract type 2008–2010	158
6.11	Decomposition employment change by work hours 2008–2010	159
7.1a	Work–family conflict: change over time by country	186
7.1b	Change in work–family conflict by unemployment rate change 2004–2010	187
7.1c	Net change in work–family conflict, controlling for work and family factors, by unemployment rate change 2004–2010	188
8.1	The characteristics of unemployment welfare systems after crisis onset	205
8.2	Share of non-financially committed population by regime, age 20–64	209
8.3	Job quality and non-financial employment commitment	210
8.4	Level and variance of non-financial employment commitment	211
8.5	Unemployment effects on non-financial employment commitment	212
8.6	Unemployment effects on non-financial employment commitment, by age	213
8.7	Unemployment effects, by unemployment rate	215
8.8	Unemployment effects, by average level of unemployment 2000–2010	215
8.9	Non-financial employment commitment, by unemployment duration	216
8.10	Job insecurity effects on non-financial employment commitment	218
8.11	Effects of job insecurity and unemployment	220
8.12	Employee downsizing and non-financial employment commitments	221
9.1	Life satisfaction scores by employment status and financial strain	236
9.2	Percentage experiencing financial strain by regime and employment situation 2010	238
9.3	Relationship between unemployment and life satisfaction before and after controls for financial situation 2010	239
9.4	Model estimated life satisfaction by regime and unemployed vs. employed 2010	241
9.5	Change in life satisfaction 2002 to 2010 (ESS Round 1 to 5)	244
9.6	Average life satisfaction in 2004 and 2010 by economic status	245
9.7	Life satisfaction changes 2004–2010 by regime and unemployment (before controls for financial stress)	246

9.8   Model estimated life satisfaction rates 2004 and 2010 by
       regime and unemployment (before controls for financial
       stress, from Model 9 in Appendix Table A9.3)   247

9.9   Life satisfaction changes 2004–2010 by regime and
       unemployment (controlling for financial stress)   247

A9.1   Mean cutbacks score by employment status and regime 2010   251

A9.2   Proportion finding it difficult or very difficult to cope on
       their present income 2004 and 2010 (Ordinary Least Squares
       Regression Coefficients)   251

10.1   The effect of GDP contraction on net average political
       trust and democratic satisfaction for the typical citizen
       by EMU membership according to Model 2 in Table 10.4   272

10.2   A Greek tragedy? Political trust and satisfaction with
       democracy in 2004 and 2010   276

List of Tables

1.1	Welfare protection for the unemployed	24
1.2	Countries and country groups	27
A1.1	Sample numbers	28
2.1	Employment fall 2007/8–2010 predicted by three factors	41
2.2	Items of scale measuring equality-promoting labour market institutions. Loadings on primary principal component, unrotated	43
3.1	Correlations between size of total employment decline 2007/8–2010 and changes in employment gaps by gender, age, and education	70
3.2	Change in earnings inequality during the recession and correlations of inequality change with recession magnitude, shifts in occupational structure, and labour market institutions	85
4.1	Logistic regression: continuing training amongst the dependently employed, pooled model	97
4.2	Net average difference *2010 versus 2004*: logit model predicting continuing training amongst the dependently employed by country	100
4.3	Macro-level determinants of change in training log odds between 2004 and 2010—Two-step estimation results (OLS)	103
4.4a	Time trends 2004–2010: net trends in educational inequality in continuing training participation amongst the dependently employed by country	105
4.4b	Time trends 2004–2010: net trends in age inequality in continuing training participation amongst the dependently employed by country	108
A4.1	Time trends 2004–2010: overall volume of continuing training amongst the dependently employed by country	111
A4.2	Macro-level variables	112
A4.3a	Predicted probabilities of training by education group and survey year	113
A4.3b	Predicted probabilities of training by age group and survey year	114

5.1	Changes in job control 2004–2010 by country group	118
5.2	Job control: year changes by class	121
5.3	Year changes in differentials by sex and contract status	122
5.4	Unemployment inflow in 2009 from the manual working classes and job control	124
5.5	Job control by financial difficulty of the firm in 2010	125
5.6	Job control in organizations experiencing financial difficulty in previous three years compared to those without financial difficulty (with controls for workforce characteristics)	125
5.7	Strength of workplace representation (mean scores) 2010	127
5.8	Employee representation and job control (with controls)	130
5.9	Bargaining coordination and strength of trade unionism (mean scores) 2000–2009	132
5.10	Changes in work intensity 2004–2010	133
5.11	Year changes in high strain jobs by class, sex, and contract status	139
6.1	Recession and probability of involuntary atypical work (odds ratios)	152
6.2	Involuntary atypical work: gender and period interactions (odds ratios)	155
6.3	Job loss by reason 2008–2010	156
6.4	Changes in subjective job insecurity and entrapment	164
6.5	Changes in the working conditions of atypical workers. Dependent variable: Had to take a pay cut	165
6.6	Risks of financial insecurity, national variations. Dependent variable: Difficult to live on household income nowadays	167
7.1a	Change over time in means, employees in couples, pooled across countries	177
7.1b	Change over time in proportion saying 'yes' on selected work and family indicators, employees in couples, pooled across eighteen countries	179
7.2a	Work–family conflict for all employees in couples, 2004 and 2010, working time and scheduling	181
7.2b	Work–family conflict for all employees in couples, 2004 and 2010, other work and family factors	183
7.3	Change over time in work–family conflict	184
7.4	The association of change in past three years with work–family conflict, 2010, accounting for other work and family factors	189
A7.1	Models of change over time in work, showing all controls	192

A7.2	Models of change over time in country differences, with and without controls	193
A7.3	Work–family conflict in 2010, including changes in work and family in past three years	194
8.1	Share of non-financially committed population by country, age 20–64	208
8.2	Country-level regressions modelling country-specific unemployment effects	214
8.3	Country-level regressions modelling country-specific insecurity effects	219
A8.1	Share of non-financially committed population by regime, age 20–64	223
A8.2	Unemployment effects, population age 20–64	224
A8.3	Predicted margins for paid work and unemployment	224
A8.4	Macro-level characteristics pertaining to unemployment	225
A8.5	Macro-level characteristics pertaining to unemployment systems	226
A8.6	Unemployment duration effects, unemployed age 20–64	227
A8.7	Effects of job insecurity, employees age 20–64	227
A8.8	Effects of job insecurity and unemployment	228
A8.9	Effects of employee downsizing, employees age 20–64	228
9.1	Social integration and employment status	239
A9.1	Poverty rates, replacement rates and benefit coverage among the unemployed	252
A9.2	Life satisfaction 2010	252
A9.3	Life satisfaction, pooled 2004–2010 model	254
10.1	OLS regressions on political attitudes: selected variables	265
10.2	The effect of introducing perceptions of the economy on time change coefficients	267
10.3	GDP contraction, net coefficients for time change (2004–2010), and 2004 values for outcome variables by country	268
10.4	Two-step regression estimates: the effect of GDP contraction and EMU membership on estimated changes in political trust, satisfaction with democracy, and attitudes towards redistribution for the typical citizen	270